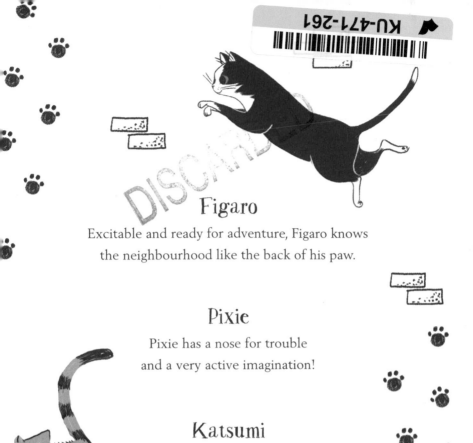

Figaro

Excitable and ready for adventure, Figaro knows
the neighbourhood like the back of his paw.

Pixie

Pixie has a nose for trouble
and a very active imagination!

Katsumi

Sleek and sophisticated,
Katsumi is quick to call Kitty
at the first sign of trouble.

For Nick Cross – P.H.

Paula, Here's to you! What a ride! – J.L.

OXFORD
UNIVERSITY PRESS

Great Clarendon Street, Oxford OX2 6DP
Oxford University Press is a department of the University of Oxford.
It furthers the University's objective of excellence in research, scholarship,
and education by publishing worldwide. Oxford is a registered trade mark
of Oxford University Press in the UK and in certain other countries

British Library Cataloguing in Publication Data

Data available

ISBN: 978-0-19-278413-1

1 3 5 7 9 10 8 6 4 2

Printed in Great Britain by Bell and Bain Ltd, Glasgow

Paper used in the production of this book is a natural,
recyclable product made from wood grown in sustainable forests.
The manufacturing process conforms to the environmental
regulations of the country of origin.

MIX
Paper from
responsible sources
FSC® C007785

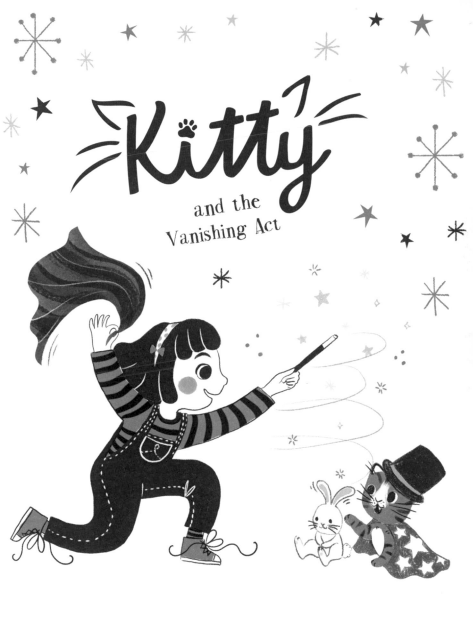

Kitty

and the
Vanishing Act

OXFORD
UNIVERSITY PRESS

Chapter
1

Kitty waved her magician's wand in
the air. Pumpkin, a small ginger kitten,
sat on the bed watching her excitedly.

'For my next trick, I will make
the rabbit reappear. Abracadabra!'
Kitty snatched away a silky black

1

handkerchief to reveal a toy rabbit underneath.

Pumpkin clapped his paws. 'That was amazing, Kitty! Show me another trick.'

Kitty beamed. Pumpkin was her best friend and they always had great fun together. She rummaged inside her magic set and pulled out an orange balloon. 'How about a magical balloon trick next?'

'Ooh, yes please!' Pumpkin scampered up and down Kitty's bed, his tiny magician's cape fluttering. A black top hat was perched lopsidedly on his head.

Kitty and Pumpkin had been playing magic tricks ever since they'd seen the posters about The Great Marella hanging outside the theatre a few days before.

The Great Marella was a famous magician who performed magic shows all over the world. She was known for her incredible conjuring tricks and her glittering costumes, and she had an animal assistant, a fluffy white poodle called Crystal. She would be performing at the Diamond Light

Theatre for the next three nights and every single show was sold-out.

Kitty blew up the orange balloon and looked at the next page in her magic book. 'You could help with this next bit, Pumpkin. It says here we should tap the balloon three times with my wand and then say the magic words—Hey Presto!'

'Imagine being a real magician's assistant!' said Pumpkin. 'It must be so scary to stand on a stage in front of hundreds of people with those bright lights shining on you.'

Kitty shrugged. 'I think some people like being the centre of attention.'

There was a sharp tapping at the window.

'Oh, what's that?' cried Pumpkin.

Kitty jumped too and her balloon burst in a cascade of golden glitter. She and Pumpkin hurried to the window and pulled back the curtain to find Figaro waiting outside.

Kitty opened the window

to let him in. 'Hello, Figaro!
You made us jump. Come
and see the magic tricks
we've been practising.'

Figaro leapt inside, his black-and-white tail quivering. 'Kitty, there's an emergency! I had to come and find you right away.'

'Oh no! What is it?' said Kitty, in alarm. 'Is Pixie in danger again? Are the alley cats causing trouble?'

'No, it's worse than that!' said

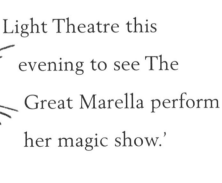

Figaro. 'I was at the Diamond Light Theatre this evening to see The Great Marella perform her magic show.'

'Ooh, what was it like?' said
Pumpkin.

Figaro smoothed his elegant black
whiskers. 'The theatre was packed and
there was an incredible atmosphere.
The lights—the music—the
costumes—well you know how much I
like the theatre, don't you? I just love a
show!'

Kitty nodded. 'But what
happened, Figaro? You said it was an
emergency.'

'Everything went well until The

Great Marella performed a vanishing trick with her poodle, Crystal,' Figaro explained. 'The little dog ran up some steps and jumped into a shiny gold box sitting on the magician's table. Then Marella waved her wand and said the magic words and—Hey Presto!—the box was empty!'

'Wasn't that supposed to happen?' said Pumpkin, looking puzzled.

'Yes, but Crystal was supposed to reappear again, and she never did,' said Figaro. 'Marella kept saying the magic

words and nothing happened. She
waved her wand hundreds of times and
then she burst into tears and ran off
the stage.'

'Poor Marella!' cried Kitty. 'So
what happened to the poodle?'

Figaro shook his head. 'No one
knows. They searched the whole
theatre from top to bottom and
she was absolutely nowhere.'

'Ooh, that's spooky!' Pumpkin
shivered.

'But dogs can't really disappear,'

said Kitty. 'Crystal must be somewhere and maybe we can help find her.'

Figaro looked pleased. 'I knew you would help! The show must go on—as they say—and Marella can't perform tomorrow night without her assistant. With your superpowers, Kitty, I bet you could find Crystal in no time!'

Spinning around, Kitty dashed to her wardrobe. 'I'll get my mask and cape right away!'

Kitty had a special secret. She was a superhero-in-training and her cat-like superpowers let her run, jump, and balance just as skilfully as a cat. She had super senses that let her see in the dark and hear sounds from a long distance away. She could also talk to animals and she'd been on many exciting moonlit adventures with her cat crew.

'Let's go to the theatre and look for clues!'

Kitty put on her mask and cape.

Then she climbed out of the window and sprang lightly on to the top of the roof.

The full moon was rising over the chimney pots. Kitty stretched up high and turned three somersaults in a row.

Her skin tingled as her superpowers grew stronger. She gazed down at the orange streetlamps lining the city streets far below. The wind stirred the trees making the leaves whisper, but most of the city lay quiet and still.

'The theatre's this way!' Kitty called back. 'It should only take us a few minutes to get there,' and she leapt to the next roof, her cape flying up in the air.

'We're right behind you, Kitty!' said Pumpkin.

The moon rose higher, pouring silvery light over the rooftops. Kitty somersaulted over a chimney pot and kept on running.

The Great Marella
must be so upset over losing
Crystal. Kitty knew she'd feel terrible
if one of her cat crew went missing. She
had to help find the little dog as fast as she
could.

'Slow down, Kitty!' gasped
Figaro. 'I can't keep up.'

Kitty stopped to wait for her friends. 'Sorry, Figaro! We're almost there now.'

They clambered down a drainpipe and hurried around a corner. Straight ahead stood a magnificent building with tall stone columns and a huge wooden door. A sign that read Diamond Light Theatre was displayed in glowing orange lights and there were posters of the upcoming shows pasted on the walls.

'But it's all locked up,' said
Pumpkin.

'We can get in up here.' Kitty
climbed onto a window ledge and
helped Figaro and Pumpkin through
an open window.

They dropped onto a grand balcony at the top of some stairs. Then they crept through the nearest doors into the back of the dark auditorium. Long rows of cushioned seats sloped down to a brightly lit stage framed by orange velvet curtains. A splendid backdrop pictured The Great Marella in her glittery costume with her dog, Crystal, beside her.

Kitty caught her breath. It was so exciting to be here inside the theatre! The place was so huge and empty that

it made her skin prickle. She imagined
Crystal vanishing in front of hundreds
of people. Where had the little dog
gone and how were they going to find
her again?

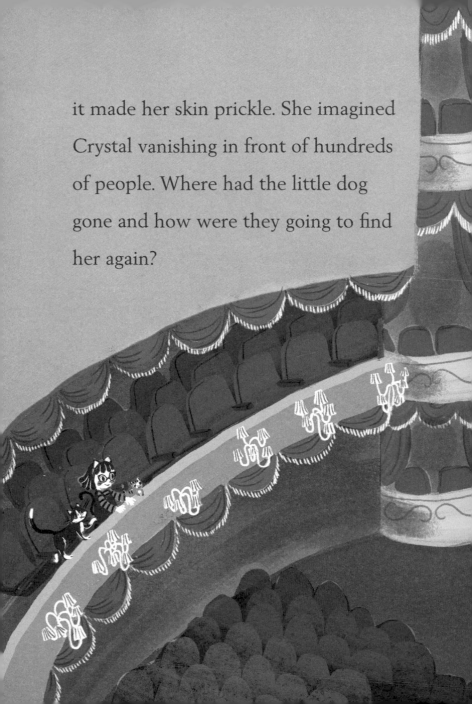

Chapter 2

Kitty peered around in the darkness. It was strange to find the theatre so quiet. She remembered coming here to see *Cinderella* the year before and the place had been full of people and laughter.

'Where is everyone?' Pumpkin whispered.

'The audience went home after Crystal vanished,' Figaro answered. 'The Great Marella ran off-stage, and no one really knew what to do. Look, there's the gold box that Crystal disappeared into.'

The shiny box sat on top of a small orange and white table in the centre of the stage.

'That's where we should start looking for clues!' Kitty ran down the aisle towards the stage, but she stopped short when someone began to sing.

A cat's voice rose in a beautiful meowing melody.

'Once upon a time, when the moon was high, and the stars twinkled in the deep, dark sky . . .' went the song. The beautiful tune filled the dark theatre.

Kitty peered around, trying to work out where the singing was coming from. Then she spotted a small cat hiding beneath Marella's table in the centre of the stage. The cat lifted her chin, singing at the top of her voice. She had ginger fur with dark splodges, almost like a leopard.

'Who's that?' said Pumpkin. 'Are they a famous singer?'

'I've never seen them before,' Figaro replied and he leaned forwards to shout at the singing cat, 'Hey you! The show finished hours ago.'

'Don't scare her away!' Kitty said quickly. 'Maybe she can help us.'

But Figaro wasn't listening. 'We need some peace and quiet,' he called over. 'Don't you know we're trying to solve a mystery here?'

The cat under the table stopped singing and her eyes widened in surprise. Then, turning tail, she ran across the stage.

'Wait!' called Kitty. 'I want to talk to you. Did you see what happened tonight?'

The spotty cat gave her a scared look and went on running. She disappeared backstage and, a moment later, the orange velvet curtains closed with a swish.

'Hold on!' cried Kitty. 'I only want to ask you some questions.' She dived under the stage curtains, but the spotty cat had already disappeared.

Everything was silent backstage. Kitty looked around for the singing cat. She searched behind piles of props and stacks of scenery. She had never been

behind the stage curtain before.

There was a wooden box full of animal

masks and a rail of costumes decorated

with sequins and feathers.

Figaro and Pumpkin wriggled

under the stage curtains.

'It's a bit spooky here.' Pumpkin
stared around, wide-eyed.

Figaro shook the dust off his
whiskers. 'Where did that cat go? She
sneaked away pretty quickly!'

Kitty put a finger to her lips. 'Shh!
I think I can hear something.'

Faint paw steps came from high

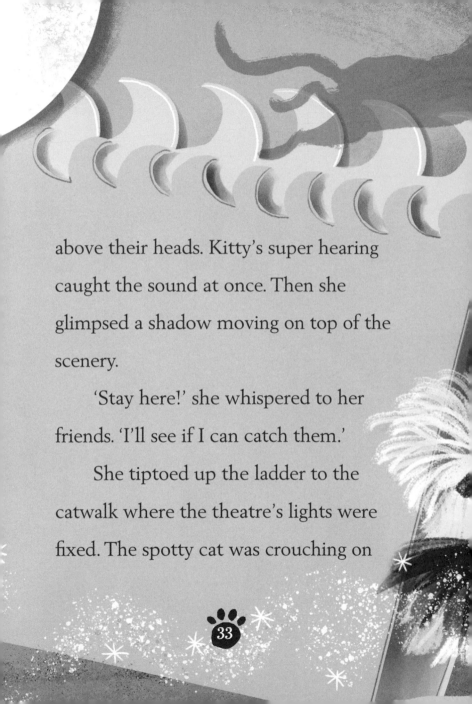

above their heads. Kitty's super hearing caught the sound at once. Then she glimpsed a shadow moving on top of the scenery.

'Stay here!' she whispered to her friends. 'I'll see if I can catch them.'

She tiptoed up the ladder to the catwalk where the theatre's lights were fixed. The spotty cat was crouching on

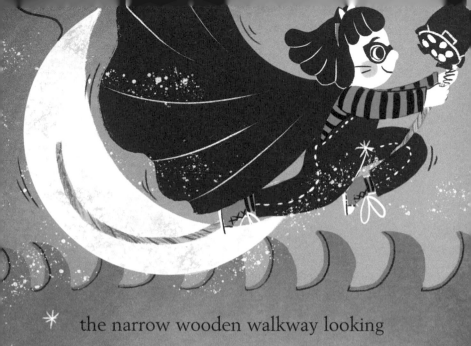

the narrow wooden walkway looking
down at Figaro and Pumpkin.

Kitty crept closer and closer.
Then she reached out her hand. 'Hello,
I'm Kitty,' she began.

The spotty cat jumped in surprise.
With a shrill meow, she leapt to the

next piece of scenery. Kitty chased after her. Her superpowers tingled as she swung from rope to rope. The theatre lights shone brightly above her.

'Come back!' she called out. 'I only want to talk to you.'

and almost lost her balance. Then
she dropped onto the catwalk and
clambered down the stage curtains.
A box of masks tumbled to the floor
with an echoing crash.

Kitty slid all the way down the
next rope and landed neatly on the
ground. She searched around quickly
but the cat had vanished again.

'She ran onto the stage!' cried
Pumpkin. 'And she knocked the masks
over so we couldn't catch up with her.'

'What a silly cat!' purred Figaro.

'She'll never outrun Kitty.'

'I don't know about that,' Kitty gasped. 'She seems to know her way around this place a lot better than I do.' Hurrying forwards, she pushed back the stage curtains.

The stage lights were dazzling. Shading her eyes, Kitty gazed out into the dark auditorium. Where had that singing cat disappeared to now?

The table in the centre of the stage wobbled and a trapdoor closed with a dull thunk as the spotty cat escaped

below the stage.

Kitty raced over and prised open the trapdoor. Then she jumped into the narrow hole and followed the steps down into the darkness.

The stairs led to a narrow tunnel and Kitty sped up when she heard paw steps ahead of her. Another flight of steps led out into a dark corridor. Kitty ran faster. The paw steps were close now. At last, she'd caught up with this disappearing cat!

She leapt forwards,
yelling, 'Found you!'

A ginger kitten stumbled
backwards.

'No, Kitty! It's only me,' said
Pumpkin.

'We ran backstage, following the
noises this way,' puffed Figaro.

Kitty stared around. Rows of doors
lined the corridor, each one marked
with a silver star. 'These must be the
dressing rooms for the performers. I bet

that cat is hiding in one of them.'

A rustling sound came from the nearest room. Kitty tiptoed to the door and opened it very slowly.

The room had a large, rectangular mirror and a dressing table covered with jewellery boxes and make-up. Glittery scarves and sequined dresses hung on a clothes rail in the corner. Behind that was a jumble of hats decorated with beads and coloured feathers. A furry orange face stared out from behind the stack of hats.

'Hello, my name's Kitty,' said Kitty, gently. 'I'm sorry if I scared you. There's really no need to worry.'

The spotty cat edged out of her hiding place. 'Why are you here? The theatre's closed right now.'

'We're trying to find Crystal, The Great Marella's assistant,' Kitty explained. 'She disappeared during the show tonight.'

The spotty cat looked surprised. 'Oh, I see! You really

scared me. I wasn't expecting anyone
to be here. So you're looking for the
poodle?'

'That's right,' Kitty said eagerly.
'We're here to hunt for clues. Did you
see what happened to her?'

The spotty cat nodded slowly. 'Yes,
I watched the whole show from up
there on top of the scenery.'

'Then you must be able to help us,'
cried Kitty. 'Were you watching closely
when The Great Marella performed
her vanishing trick? Did you see what

happened next?'

'I saw everything,' the cat replied. 'And I know exactly how that poodle disappeared.'

Chapter 3

Figaro padded closer and studied the spotty cat suspiciously. 'Just a minute! Who ARE you and how do you know this place so well?'

'I live here!' said the spotty cat. 'I wandered inside one freezing cold

night when I was a stray kitten. I found
a wonderful place to sleep in a box of
warm scarves in the storeroom and I've
been living here ever since. My name's
Dusty.'

'Nice to meet you, Dusty,' said
Kitty. 'I loved your singing. You must
practice on the stage quite a lot.'

Dusty covered her face with
her paws. 'Oh dear! I wouldn't have
started singing if I'd known someone
was here.'

'Were you pretending to be a star? Everyone daydreams about stardom from time to time!' Figaro leapt onto the dressing table and preened his whiskers in front of the mirror.

'I'll never be a star—my fur is too ragged and my tail's too short,' sighed Dusty. 'But I love singing—even without an audience. I always wait until everyone's gone home before I begin.'

'I thought you sounded wonderful,' said Pumpkin.

Dusty brightened. 'Thank you!'

'It's lucky you know the theatre so well,' said Kitty. 'Can you tell us what happened to Crystal tonight? Has she found a secret hiding place backstage?'

Dusty shook her head. 'No, I'm afraid not. I watched the vanishing trick closely. Crystal should have come back up through the trapdoor onto the stage. When she didn't reappear, I climbed down and checked around backstage. I saw Crystal dashing out of the backstage door and disappearing into the night.'

'Really?' Kitty's eyes widened. 'But why would she leave The Great Marella in the middle of the show?'

'I don't know, but that poodle is quite a diva,' Dusty said disapprovingly.

'She was strutting around before the show wanting more and more dog treats. When the treats ran out, she got in a really bad temper.'

'Dear me!' sniffed Figaro. 'I do hate it when creatures act all spoilt.'

'Can you show us where she disappeared?' Kitty said eagerly. 'Maybe it'll help us work out where she's gone.'

'Of course! Follow me.' Dusty hurried out of the dressing-room and raced down the corridor onto the stage. She jumped onto the table in the centre

of the stage and
placed her paw on the
glittering gold box.
Kitty peered inside
the box and was surprised to
see a hole in the bottom.
'The box and the table have

a secret opening. Crystal hid inside like this!' Dusty jumped into the box. 'Then she disappeared through the trapdoor. She was meant to reappear on the stage and surprise everyone.'

'Where did she go?' asked Pumpkin.

'She ran this way.' Dusty led them to a little backstage door.

Kitty opened the door and looked outside. A gust of wind sent fallen leaves whirling down the alleyway.

It was dark and cold, and there was no sign of Crystal.

Figaro tutted crossly. 'She could be anywhere by now.'

'Marella cried and cried after she left,' said Dusty.

'We have to find Crystal right away,' said Kitty. 'She doesn't know her way around Hallam City and she shouldn't be out there all alone. You will help us, won't you Dusty? You've seen Crystal up close, and you know what she looks like.'

Dusty shrank back. 'I don't go out very often. I like to stay here where it's cosy.'

'I know how you feel!' said Pumpkin.

'It takes a lot of bravery to step outside when you feel safe and warm at home.'

'I'll make sure you're all right,' said Figaro, patting Dusty in a kindly manner.

'It would really help us if you came along,' Kitty added.

'Well . . . all right then.' Dusty took a deep breath and gingerly stepped out of the door.

Kitty began to climb up the nearest drainpipe. 'Let's try the rooftop. Maybe we'll spot Crystal from there!'

The clouds cleared
away as Kitty and
the cats climbed onto
the high theatre roof.
Moonlight poured down,
glinting on the river in
the distance, and the stars
overhead shone like diamonds.

Kitty searched the streets
below, using her superpowered
eyesight to see in the dark.
She spotted the shops, the

park and the museum. She could even see her own house a few streets away, but she couldn't see Crystal.

'Just look at all the stars!' Dusty said dreamily. 'I forgot how beautiful it is out here.'

'Look, there's a white poodle!' cried Pumpkin. 'Oh, no it isn't!

It's just a paper bag.'

    'Wait! I can hear paw steps.' Kitty peered at the alleyway below.

    Katsumi, a graceful tabby cat, ran along the alley and climbed swiftly up to the theatre roof.

'Hello, Katsumi,' said Kitty. 'Are you looking for us?'

'Yes, I was sure it was you up here,' Katsumi replied. 'Can I ask your advice, Kitty?'

'Of course you can.' Kitty touched foreheads with the tabby cat. She wondered what could be wrong. Katsumi was so sensible that she hardly ever needed help or advice.

'Pixie and I were walking in the park when we found a little white dog looking ever so lost,' Katsumi explained.

'She barked at us—saying she didn't want any help—but she seems really unhappy, and we can't work out what's wrong.'

'That could be Crystal!' Kitty saw Katsumi's puzzled look. 'I'll explain on the way,' she called back, dashing across the rooftop.

The cats hurried after Kitty. Figaro waited for Dusty and checked she was all right.

Kitty leapt from roof to roof as lightly as a moonbeam. Her cloak fluttered in the wind. In the distance, she could hear Pixie shouting. Her stomach turned over. Something sounded very wrong.

'I'll meet you there!' she told the others. Then she raced to the edge of the roof and sprang into the air. Catching hold of a lamppost, she slid all the way to the ground.

'Woof WOOF! AROO!'
A panicked yowling and barking came from the park.

Kitty rushed down the street and

leapt over the park gate. She hesitated for a moment, wondering which path to choose.

'Quick—somebody help!' mewed Pixie.

Kitty raced through the bushes and stopped beside a moonlit pond. Pixie was standing on the other side, staring up into a tall tree. Clutching onto a narrow branch near the top, was a fluffy white poodle.

Pixie spotted Kitty and leapt up and down. 'Over here, Kitty! That dog's got stuck and she doesn't

know what to do.'

A sharp gust of wind

rocked the tree, and the

poodle gave a frightened

yelp.

'Hold on, Crystal!' Kitty

felt a rush of superpowers as

she started to run.

Chapter

4

Kitty raced around the pond, her cloak flying out behind her. She could see Crystal clutching onto a branch with her paws. Another gust of wind shook the tree, sending leaves whirling through the air.

'Help me! I'm going to fall,' the poodle yelped.

'Don't worry! I'll get you down,' cried Kitty, running faster and faster.

Crystal clung to the tree, her tail trembling. The wind grew rougher, and the tree swayed like a boat on the ocean. Clusters of leaves blew off the branches and spun through the air. Crystal whimpered and tried to edge back along the branch, but it swung dangerously.

'Quickly, Kitty!' urged Pixie.

'I can't reach her myself.'

Kitty took a run up and leapt high in the air, grabbing hold of a low branch. From there, she swung herself up the tree.

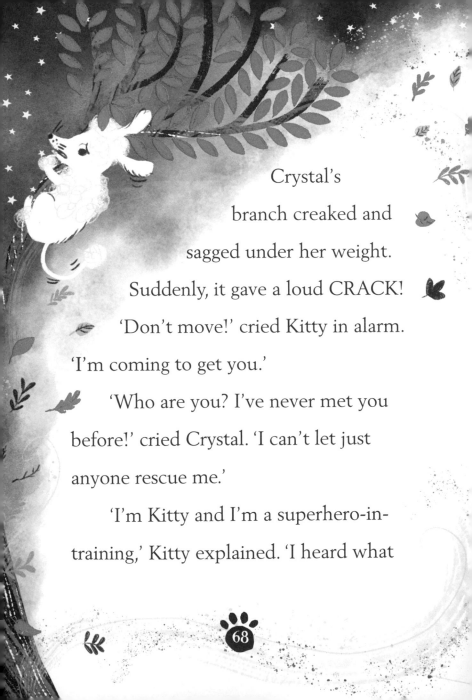

Crystal's
branch creaked and
sagged under her weight.
Suddenly, it gave a loud CRACK!
'Don't move!' cried Kitty in alarm.
'I'm coming to get you.'

'Who are you? I've never met you
before!' cried Crystal. 'I can't let just
anyone rescue me.'

'I'm Kitty and I'm a superhero-in-
training,' Kitty explained. 'I heard what

happened at your magic show and I came to find you. Please let me help!'

'It's not fair!' sniffed Crystal. 'Everything's gone wrong today. I WISH I'd never come to this horrible city.'

The branch creaked again. Then suddenly, it snapped.

Crystal yapped in terror as she fell. Kitty swung up from the branch below. She reached out, but the poodle slipped past her fingers.

'AROO!' howled Crystal, as she tumbled through the air.

Pixie dived out of the way.

The poodle fell faster and faster.

SPLASH! She fell right into the pond,

spraying water everywhere.

Kitty jumped down and ran

to the water's edge. Crystal was

floundering in the water and her fur
was tangled with pondweed. Kitty
sprang lightly onto a floating log.
She pulled the little dog from the
water before leaping to the bank.

'Nice rescue, Kitty!' called Pixie.

The poodle shook herself,
splattering Kitty with water.

Kitty undid her cape and offered
it to Crystal. 'Are you OK? You can dry
yourself on my cape if you like.'

'Oh, thank you!' Crystal burst into
yapping sobs.

Kitty crouched down beside her.

'What's wrong? Do
you hate getting
wet?'

'It's so cold!' shuddered Crystal. 'I only like water when it's a warm lavender-scented bath with extra bubbles like the one Marella makes me.'

'That sounds lovely,' said Kitty.

Crystal sobbed even harder. 'It IS lovely! Marella always looks after me. Why was I such a naughty dog? I miss my cosy hotel room and my soft doggie bed. I miss my bone-shaped biscuits and I miss Marella most of all!'

'Then why did you run away from the theatre tonight?' asked Kitty.

'You left Marella right in the middle of your vanishing trick.'

Crystal stared down at her paws. 'I wanted everyone to pay me more attention! Marella's the great magician so she gets all the applause. I thought if I disappeared for the rest of the show it would prove how important I was—after all the trick doesn't work without me! But then I got lost. There are so many streets in this city, and they all look the same. I got splashed with muddy water when a lorry went past and now my coat looks disgusting.'

Kitty wiped Crystal's messy coat. 'Hallam City's a really big place. It's easy to get lost if you don't know the way.'

Mewing voices echoed across the park. Kitty swung round and spotted Dusty and the others making their way around the pond. Pixie ran to meet them.

Katsumi bounded straight over to Kitty. 'What happened? The little dog was safe on dry land when I left.'

Pixie coughed. 'That was really my fault. I was trying to cheer her up, so I talked about all the things cats can do better than dogs—like climbing and balancing and—well everything really! Then she climbed up that tree to prove I was wrong.'

'Oh Pixie!' Figaro tutted. 'I don't think that was the best way to cheer Crystal up. It was sure to end in disaster!'

Crystal jumped up and shook herself again. 'I know you all think I'm

just a silly puppy, but
you don't know how hard it
is performing all around the world!
I get so tired and—' She broke off as a
sweet tune floated through the night air.
Dusty had climbed onto a park
bench. Lifting her whiskers, she sang
her beautiful song about a
starry night.

The music swirled around them
as it floated into the night sky.
Kitty and the others listened,
spellbound, and when Dusty had
finished, they all clapped eagerly.

'Encore!' shouted Figaro.
'Take a bow, Dusty.'

Dusty looked shy. 'I'm sorry
everyone! It's been a long time
since I came out at night and the

beautiful starlit sky made me want to sing.'

'You sounded very good!' said Crystal in surprise. 'Do you ever sing at the Diamond Light Theatre?'

'Only when it's empty,' Dusty explained. 'I'd be too shy to perform all by myself in front of hundreds of people.'

'That's what's nice about MY show,' cried Crystal. 'I'm never alone! I always perform next to Marella.' She suddenly looked sad. 'I really miss her!'

'Why don't you go and make friends again?' Kitty said gently. 'I bet she'll be happy to see you! She must be so worried.'

Crystal's tail drooped. 'But I'm so embarrassed! I NEVER should have run off like that. I'm the silliest poodle in the world!'

'Let's go back and find her right

now,' said Kitty. 'Which hotel are you staying at?'

'The Sunningdale Hotel. But I don't know where that is.' Crystal's nose quivered. 'I'm completely lost!'

'I think I know where it is. Follow me!' Kitty waved goodbye to Pixie and Katsumi and led the others out of the park. She scooped up Crystal and climbed to the rooftops with Figaro, Pumpkin, and Dusty close behind her.

The moon had risen high in the dark sky. Kitty studied the streets below, looking for the hotel. At last, she spotted a tall building a few streets along. Gigantic letters at the top of the building spelt The Sunningdale Hotel.

Kitty hurried across the rooftops

and jumped onto the hotel roof with Crystal in her arms.

Crystal wagged her tail. 'My room is just down there! It's the one with the plants on the balcony.'

Kitty swung down to the balcony and tapped on the glass door. When no one answered, she slid the door open and climbed inside. The room was full of magician's equipment from hats and cloaks to magic wands. On a silver perch in the corner, sat a dark-eyed parrot with beautiful orange-and-blue wings.

'Where's Marella?' cried Crystal. 'I thought she'd be waiting for me.'

'SQUAWK! She's gone looking for you,' screeched the parrot, fluffing out his feathers. 'She was too worried to sleep, so she went back to the theatre to search for you all over again.'

Crystal's tail drooped. 'Poor Marella! I'm sorry I've caused so much trouble.'

'We can go back to the theatre to meet her. Hold on tight!' Kitty settled Crystal on her shoulder and climbed back onto the balcony. Then, calling to her friends, she rushed off into the moonlit night.

Chapter 5

Kitty and her cat crew

hurried back across the rooftops as fast
as they could. They stopped on the roof
of the Diamond Light Theatre to catch
their breath.

'Do you think Marella's really

here?' asked Crystal. 'What if I can't find her?'

Figaro peered over the edge of the roof. 'There's a fabulous white limousine parked right outside the door. That must be The Great Marella's car. It's too grand to belong to anyone else.'

'Let's go and find out,' Kitty said, smiling.

Crystal scampered forward eagerly. Then she stopped, her tail drooping. 'I can't go down there! Running away in the middle of the show was a TERRIBLE thing to do. I don't think I deserve to be Marella's assistant anymore.'

'But you're so good on stage,' said Dusty. 'You gave an amazing performance tonight.'

Crystal wagged her tail. 'I do love being on the stage! I get a rush of energy when the curtains draw back and I see the faces of the audience.'

'There's nowhere as wonderful as the theatre,' Dusty agreed. 'This place has a special smell—it's the wooden polish mixed with the scent of the make-up. And when the audience laugh or gasp at exactly the same time, it's like magic!'

'But what if Marella won't forgive me?' sniffed Crystal. 'She might not want to see me again.'

'She doesn't sound like the sort of person who would break a friendship over one mistake,' said Pumpkin.

'You should go and find her,' urged Kitty.

'I guess you're right! Could you

take me down there, Kitty?' asked Crystal.

Putting the poodle on her shoulders, Kitty climbed down the drainpipe. Then she lifted Crystal through the first-floor window and they hurried into the dark theatre. Crystal stopped suddenly and stared down at the stage.

The Great Marella was standing all alone in the centre of the stage under the beam of a single spotlight. She looked very different from the

glamorous figure on the
posters. She was dressed
in orange check
pyjamas and bunny
slippers as if she
had been
getting
ready for
bed.

She opened the golden box lying on the table—the prop for the show's vanishing trick. Then she sighed deeply and rubbed her eyes.

Kitty crouched beside Crystal. 'You should go down there,' she whispered. 'I'm sure she's longing to see you.'

'You're right. I must be brave!' Crystal pricked up her ears. Then she hurtled down the aisle like a fluffy white whirlwind. With a loud bark, she bounded straight onto the stage.

Marella gasped when she saw the little poodle. 'CRYSTAL!' she shrieked. 'I've been looking for you EVERYWHERE!'

'Woof WOOF!' barked Crystal, leaping up and down.

Marella knelt down and checked Crystal all over. 'Are you sure you're not hurt? Or hungry? I was worried that you might have got lost somewhere!'

The little poodle wagged her tail joyfully and licked Marella's ear. Then she scampered round and round the magician's feet.

Marella beamed and swept Crystal into an enormous hug. 'I missed you so much! Let's go back to the hotel and have some of your favourite bone-shaped biscuits.'

'WOOF!' agreed Crystal.

Kitty smiled. It was lovely to see them reunited again. She quietly left the theatre and clambered back out of the window. Climbing down a drainpipe, she found her friends in the alleyway. Dusty was leading them through the little backstage door.

'Dusty's going to show us around backstage,' Figaro explained. 'And then take us to the theatre restaurant for a delicious supper!'

Dusty showed them her cosy nest

in the storeroom and the place on top of the scenery where she liked to watch every show. Then she took them up to the theatre restaurant on the second floor.

Kitty looked around the kitchen and found some chocolate milkshake for herself and some fresh fishcakes for her cat friends. Then she left plenty of coins on the counter to pay for it all.

She caught a glimpse of Marella and Crystal climbing into the white limousine parked outside. Crystal

jumped up and down on the backseat
of the car, her tail wagging happily.

Pumpkin leaned his paws against
the window as he looked down at the
street. 'Crystal and Marella are best
friends again. Just like you and me,
Kitty!'

'And tomorrow night's show has been saved,' added Figaro.

'But why wasn't Marella angry with Crystal?' said Dusty. 'After all, she did run away and spoil the show.'

'I think everyone makes mistakes,' said Kitty. 'And sometimes you have to give a friend a second chance, especially if they've said they're sorry.'

Dusty nodded. 'I guess you're right. Everyone makes mistakes sometimes.'

Figaro finished off his fishcake and wiped his whiskers. 'I'd love to hear your beautiful song one more time, dear Dusty. Do you think you'll ever sing it to a real audience on the stage?'

'Oh no! That sounds much too scary,' said Dusty. 'I'm sure no one wants to listen to me singing.'

'But you're a magnificent singer!' cried Figaro. 'You really MUST start believing in yourself.'

'I used to feel nervous about

singing in front of people too,' said
Kitty. 'Maybe you could try singing for
a few people at first and see how that
goes. Didn't it feel amazing singing in
the park tonight?'

'Yes it did!' Dusty brightened.

'And you were all very kind. I guess I could try singing for just a few people.'

'And you must come and have supper with us tomorrow,' cried Figaro. 'There's so much more I want to ask you about the theatre and all the famous people you've met.'

Kitty noticed Pumpkin yawning. 'We ought to head home now, but why don't we come to collect you tomorrow? I'll buy some food and we can have a party on my rooftop at home.'

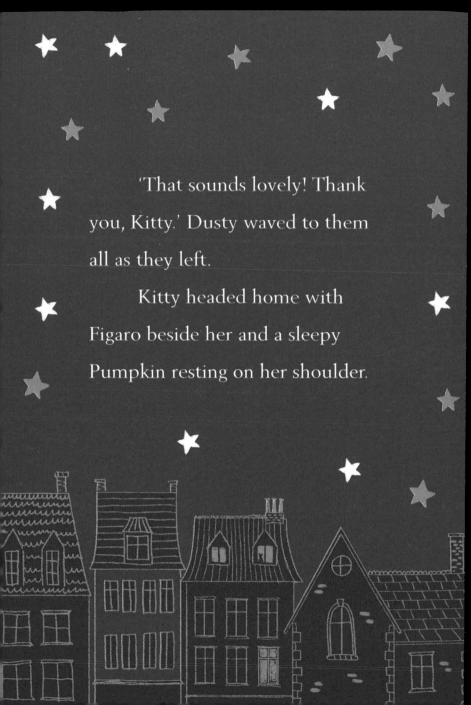

'That sounds lovely! Thank you, Kitty.' Dusty waved to them all as they left.

Kitty headed home with Figaro beside her and a sleepy Pumpkin resting on her shoulder.

She turned back before climbing through her bedroom window. She could just make out the sparkling theatre lights in the distance, shining in the darkness like a flock of stars.

Chapter 6

'All right everyone! Are you ready?' said Kitty, waving her magician's wand excitedly.

She was standing in front of her cat friends on the flat rooftop above her bedroom window. Pumpkin skipped up and down beside her, dressed in his little magician's cape and top hat.

Figaro and Dusty had come for a midnight feast along with Crystal, who had finished performing for the night. Katsumi and Pixie had come along too. Fairy lights twinkled around the rooftop and there was a picnic rug in the middle piled with fishcakes and salmon slices for the cats, and blueberry muffins for Kitty.

Kitty waved her wand again and tried to remember how the magic trick went. She had been practising all afternoon and she wanted to get it just right. Crystal wagged her tail and gave a little bark of encouragement.

'I will now make Pumpkin

disappear!' Kitty declared. 'As you can see, this bag is completely empty. Now Pumpkin! Jump in please.'

Pumpkin leapt inside the bag and snuggled down at the bottom.

Kitty waved her wand over the bag. 'Abracadabra, dippitty day. Make this kitten vanish right away!'

Pumpkin scrambled out of the secret hole in the bottom of the bag. Then he crept behind Kitty and tunnelled underneath the picnic rug.

Kitty showed the audience the inside of the bag. 'And as you can see, Pumpkin has vanished and the bag is empty again.'

'Ooh, he's really disappeared,' said Figaro. 'Where's he gone, Kitty?'

'I will work my magic and show you!' Kitty twirled her magic wand. 'Abracadabra pippitty pow. Make the kitten appear right now!'

'MEOW!' Pumpkin leapt out from behind Kitty like magic.

Everyone cheered and mewed all at once.

'That was very good, Kitty!' Crystal said approvingly. 'With a bit more practice you'll be a really fantastic magician.'

'Thanks, Crystal!' Kitty beamed.

'And now I'm going to invite a very special cat to sing. Dusty would you like to come to the front?'

Dusty crept forwards reluctantly. 'Are you sure this is a good idea?' she whispered to Kitty. 'What if I go wrong?'

'Just do your best!' Kitty whispered back. 'Your song sounds lovely.'

Dusty stared around with wide eyes. Then, at last, she began to sing. Her sweet voice drifted over the rooftop and floated into the moonlit sky.

Kitty smiled as she listened.

When Dusty had finished, Kitty and the others cheered loudly.

'Bravo!' called Figaro. 'Your singing is even more amazing than these salmon slices.'

'Figaro's right! It sounded great,' said Kitty. 'You should be very proud of yourself.'

'Thank you!' Dusty said shyly. 'I've been practising that song a lot.'

'You could perform in a show if you wanted to,' Crystal told her.

'Imagine touring the world and singing to hundreds of people all at once. You could become a star!'

Dusty shook her head. 'I'm much happier just singing to all of you. It's wonderful to have met such lovely new friends.'

'Friendship is more important than stardom,' Figaro said wisely. 'In fact, it's even more important than fishcakes!'

Super Facts About Cats

Super Speed

Have you ever seen a cat make a quick escape from a dog? If so, you'll know that they can move *really* fast—up to 30mph!

Super Hearing

Cats have an incredible sense of hearing and can swivel their large ears to pinpoint even the tiniest of sounds.

Super Reflexes

Have you ever heard the saying 'cats always land on their feet'? People say this because cats have amazing reflexes. If a cat is falling, they can sense quickly how to move their bodies into the right position to land safely.

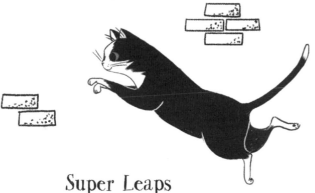

Super Leaps

A cat can jump over eight feet high
in a single leap; this is due to its powerful
back leg muscles.

Super Vision

Cats have amazing night-time vision. Their
incredible ability to see in low light allows them
to hunt for prey when it's dark outside.

Super Smell

Cats have a very powerful sense of smell,
14 times stronger than a human's. Did you know
that the pattern of ridges on each cat's nose
is as unique as a human's fingerprint?

About the author

Paula Harrison

Before launching a successful writing career,
Paula was a Primary school teacher. Her years teaching
taught her what children like in stories and how
they respond to humour and suspense. She went on
to put her experience to good use, writing many
successful stories for young readers.

About the illustrator

Jenny Løvlie

Jenny is a Norwegian illustrator, designer,
creative, foodie, and bird enthusiast. She is fascinated
by the strong bond between humans and animals and
loves using bold colours and shapes in her work.

Love Kitty?
Why not try these too . . .